Copyright © 2020 Shawniece Moore.

All rights reserved. No part of this publication may be reproduced, distributed, or transmitted in any form or by any means, including photocopying, recording, or other electronic or mechanical methods, without the prior written permission of the publisher, except in the case of brief quotations embodied in critical reviews and certain other noncommercial uses permitted by copyright law. For permission requests, write to the publisher, addressed "Attention: Permissions Coordinator," at the address below.

ISBN: 978-0-578-70285-8 (Paperback)

Cover design by: Tyrone Rose

Editor: Dr. Kristie Searcy, Class A Editing

Printed in the United States of America

First printing edition 2020.

Uniquely Complex, LLC

Richmond, VA

www.uniquelycomplex.com

TABLE OF CONTENTS

ACKNOWLEDGMENTS V

FORWARD VII

INTRODUCTION 1

DAY 1- UNIQUELY COMPLEX 4

DAY 2- YOU ARE A MASTERPIECE 7

DAY 3- I MATTER 10

DAY 4- THE STRUGGLE 13

DAY 5- I'M SLIPPING 17

DAY 6- HIS GRACE 20

DAY 7- HIS MERCY 23

DAY 8- SAFE PLACE 26

DAY 9- DEVELOPING ENDURANCE 29

DAY 10- FAITH AND ENDURANCE 33

DAY 11- HAVE HOPE 37

DAY 12- CONSTRUCTIVE CRITICISM 41

DAY 13- DISCIPLINE 44

DAY 14- HE PROMISED ME 47

DAY 15- HOW HE LOVES ME SO 51

DAY 16- GOD REMEMBERED ME 54

DAY 17- YOU ARE TREASURED 57

DAY 18- SOUL TIES 60

DAY 19- SAVING MYSELF 64

DAY 20- OVERFLOW OF HIS LOVE 67

DAY 21- HE RESCUED ME 70

DAY 22- PLANS FOR ME 73

DAY 23- YOUR TRUE SELF 77

DAY 24- I GOT THE POWER 81

DAY 25- HATE ON ME 84

DAY 26- I'VE GOT CONFIDENCE 87

DAY 27- SPEAK INTO MY LIFE 90

DAY 28- LIVE IN PEACE 93

DAY 29- I GOT THE VICTORY 96

DAY 30 - FUTURE GLORY **99**

APPENDIX A **103**

ABOUT THE AUTHOR **105**

REFERENCES **106**

Acknowledgments

This devotional would not have been possible without my husband, Dr. Chris L. Moore Sr. I am a procrastinator to an extent. When it is something to better myself, I take my time. But one night during the Covid-19 Pandemic, he asked me to talk about goal mapping during our virtual bible study; 30-day goals for people to work on. Well, I had to lead by example, so I vowed to finish this devotional over the next 30 days. He also inspired the title of this devotional, so I am so grateful and love him with my whole heart for pushing me and seeing the potential in me when I didn't.

I also want to thank my daughter, Montae, who I truly value because she doesn't hold back her feedback. When she was captured by my introduction and 1st day of the devotional, I knew this was it. I am so blessed and humbled to have a wonderful church family who has always embraced me and supported my brand Uniquely Complex. New Kingdom Christian Ministries, I love you dearly and thank you for all your prayers. The Virtuous Women of Faith have pushed me to be a better me to be able to help them and mold them into their purpose.

I also want to thank my spiritual parents Dr. R.A. and Dr. Victory Vernon. Their teaching and genuine love for my husband and me is indescribable. Their support means the world to me. A special thank you to Dr. Victory Vernon for providing the foreword to this baby of mine. She is truly a gem, and a great example of what a Proverbs 31 woman is. I love you to the moon and back.

Forward

Dr. Victory Vernon

Shawniece is a woman called into ministry with the unmatched gift to reach God's people. She is a true champion for Christ, who has now researched, pinned, and dedicated a book that will inspire many to commune with God and His Word. Shawniece has implored the human heart that time with Christ is essential. If you're like me and have a mission to develop and sustain a closer relationship with your creator, allow this easy devotional to minister to your heartstrings and give you the guidance you need to accomplish such a worthwhile goal. Anyone who is searching for an effective daily walk through God's garden of rich love, comfort, joy, healing, and restoration should read this devotional as a resource.

God's redemptive work, mercy, and grace are available with each new dawning, and Shawniece has invited us to feed off His word for a unique experience every day.

Psalms 34:8 (NIV) says, Taste and see that the Lord is good; blessed is the one that takes refuge in him. If you add this ideal to your spiritual formation, your life will never be the same. Hold on to His word daily and trust in His promises. Thank you Shawniece for being courageous enough to accept the assignment and take us on a daily walk with the only one who has all the answers.

Introduction

Who would ever think I would be the one to encourage, motivate, and push women to boost their self-esteem? As a little girl, I battled with low self-esteem until my mid-30s. It stemmed from being bullied in elementary school. Unfortunately, it was girls of my own race that would pick on me and start fights. It could be because I was quiet, because of my hair, or my shape. I will never really know, but it affected me in a major way. It caused me to be very defensive, quick to argue, and very short-tempered throughout the years. It even caused me to look for affirmation in men. I grew up in a two-parent household. My dad loved and adored me, but he worked nights and was in the Air Force Reserve. My mom was there, but she showed little affection because of the way she grew up. This created a void for me. I found myself seeking attention from men.

Several years ago, I discovered God had plans for me I never expected. It is one of those things where you are like a college sports player, ready to go to the next professional level, whether it be the NBA, WNBA, NFL, etc. You enter the draft, hoping you get selected for the team of your dreams. But instead, you end up getting drafted to a team you didn't expect. I always imagined I would get married, have a successful career, and live happily ever after. I never imagined a call to ministry and speaking life into women. Like some players, I thought the other team is where I should be, but once I started playing for the team that picked me, I realized I didn't want to be anywhere else.

In 2014, I married the love of my life. At the time, he was a youth Pastor, which was not much to really live up to, in my opinion. Being the wife of a Youth Pastor didn't require a lot of my time. I could sit where I wanted to sit when at church and was only committed to stay after church on certain Sundays. We had our personal life that wasn't on public display. And honestly, I enjoyed the fact that I only had to talk to who I wanted to talk to. It all changed when he had to become Senior Pastor, and I became the "First" Lady of the church. This was a team I didn't expect to get drafted to. Things started to shift emotionally, spiritually, and mentally. It went from choosing to go to certain functions to having to go to ALL functions. I could no longer choose my conversations because I now had to deal with ALL the people.

That kind of pressure and expectation brought on uncertainty in my ability to lead. I was particularly concerned about interacting with the women; what exactly should I or shouldn't I do; what should I or should I not wear? I became so confused as to who I should be compared to who I was already. I had dealt with low self-esteem for quite some time. I remember thinking that I knew what I wanted out of life and where I was headed. But that all changed when I became the First Lady. In February 2018, our church went on a corporate fast. My focus was to discover my God-given purpose. I was in a full-time job that paid good money, but I was miserable. I came to realize it was because I was not doing what I was supposed to be doing. While reading a book called, "She is Still Here" by Crystal Evans-Hurst, I read one of the scriptures she presented. Psalms 139:13-14 states "You made all the delicate, inner parts of my body and knit me together in my mother's womb. Thank you for making me so wonderfully complex! Your workmanship is marvelous—how well I know it." After reading that scripture and journaling about my struggles with my own identity and purpose, God gave me Uniquely Complex.

This name and brand are designed to motivate and encourage women to defeat self-doubt and walk in their purpose. My prayer is that this 30-day devotional will help you on your self-love journey through scripture, testimonies, and forward-thinking questions. Let this make you do a self-evaluation, dig deep and find that girl, that woman God has called you to be. Each day after your devotional, you will have to write a self-affirmation or declaration over your life. By the end of this devotional, you will have a list of positive words, phrases, and affirmations that describe your best you! Make sure you take that list and post it somewhere you will see it daily. So, let's get started on this self-love journey!

Day 1- Uniquely Complex

"Thank you for making me so wonderfully complex! Your workmanship is marvelous—how well I know it." Psalms 139:14 New Living Translation Version

I sometimes look in the mirror and am reminded of all my flaws. No matter how much I try to ignore the flaws or tell myself I'm amazing, self-doubt creeps in, and once again, the quest for perfection steals my joy.

But then I remember, no one is perfect. We all have a unique attribute about ourselves, but we must be willing to accept and embrace it. We all have a distinct fingerprint as no one is the same. That's where uniqueness comes in. As women, we are very complex creatures. Our bodies go through so many changes in different phases of our lives. One minute we can be happy, the next minute sad. One-minute we are mad with someone, and the next minute be filled with compassion. Although these are normal emotions for most women, how can we channel those emotions to a place that works for our good? I have always been a very emotional person. This has been both a good and bad thing. I stated in my introduction that I was quick to argue and be defensive. Earlier life experiences caused these emotions, but I had to learn how to disseminate that energy in a different way while still staying true to my authentic self. It took years to become self-aware and shift my emotions to a place of love and self-care.

Can you handle the fact that you are different, all while controlling your emotions?   As today's scripture reads, His workmanship is marvelous! God doesn't make mistakes, so you are not one! He also does not expect you to be mean, disrespectful, and unloving. He has a purpose for you, and that's why you were created in His image. Look in the mirror and know God made a work of art! He wants you to be your best self. He doesn't look for perfection as the formal definition of art is "the expression or application of creative skill and imagination, typically in a visual form such as painting or sculpture, producing works to be appreciated primarily for their beauty or emotional power." That last part should make your heart smile. God produced a work (you) to be appreciated for your beauty and emotional power. So let your beauty and power be seen by all as God is smiling down on you.

"Remember always that you not only have the right to be an individual, you have an obligation to be one."
– Eleanor Roosevelt

Self-Reflections

What do you know about God that tells you what He thinks about you?

_____
_____
_____

_____
_____
_____
_____

When do you feel like your best?
_____
_____
_____
_____
_____
_____
_____
_____

Positive self-declaration/affirmation for today:
_____
_____
_____

Prayer
Lord, I thank you for making me so wonderfully complex! My complexity helps me to stand out from the rest. As I start the daily self- love devotional, my prayer is that my heart posture and my mindset is transformed in a positive way. In Jesus' name, Amen.

Day 2- You are a Masterpiece

We are God's masterpiece. He has created us anew in Christ Jesus, so we can do the good things he planned for us long ago."
Ephesians 2:10 New Living Translation Version

Yesterday we talked about you being his workmanship, embracing the unique person He has created. Well, you are also His masterpiece in which he has a purpose planned for you. Webster's Dictionary defines a masterpiece as a work done with extraordinary skill.

You can create a piece of your masterpiece every day. That is your purpose. My husband did a bible study/sermon series on purpose. A few statements he said stuck out to me. "Every day we are given, it is a chance to put a piece of your purpose into place," and "Every piece of the puzzle fits somewhere. Don't try to figure out the whole picture; work on each piece at a time." The premise of his lesson was don't overwhelm yourself with the end results. Focus on what you must work with today. Each day is a piece to put towards your purpose.

The Passion Translation Version says, "We have become his poetry, a re-created people that will fulfill the destiny he has given each of us, for we are joined to Jesus, the Anointed One. Even before we were born, God planned in advance our destiny and the good works we would do to fulfill it!" You were made with a purpose in mind, and you will fulfill that purpose. The main part of this version that stands out is that God planned in **advance** our destiny. This should spark something in you to know God had a plan for your life before you were even born. It is your job to carry out what He has put inside you. Don't fret, He is there to help and guide you, but you have to be willing to let Him do so.

"Self-improvement without self-love is like building a house upon sand. You can build and build, but it will always sink."
— **Vironika Tugaleva, The Love Mindset: An Unconventional Guide to Healing and Happiness**

Self-Reflections

What is my definition of purpose?

_____
_____
_____
_____
_____
_____

What piece can I add today that will help create my masterpiece?

_____
_____
_____

_____
_____
_____

Positive self-declaration/affirmation for today:
_____
_____
_____
_____

Prayer

Lord, give me THIS day, My daily bread. Please help me and guide me in the path I need to go to appreciate me, your masterpiece. I want to appreciate your mighty work so I can then start working to put together the pieces of my purpose to make a masterpiece here on earth. In Jesus' name, Amen.

Day 3- I Matter

"I pray that your love will overflow more and more and that you will keep on growing in knowledge and understanding. For I want you to understand what really matters, so that you may live pure and blameless lives until the day of Christ's return." Philippians 1:9-10 New Living Translation Version

In his book, "The 7 Habits of Highly Effective People" Stephen Covey talks about a principle-centered, character-based, "inside-out" approach to personal and interpersonal effectiveness. The inside-out approach says that private victories precede public victories, that making and keeping promises to ourselves precedes making and keeping promises to others.

The problem is, most of us are naturally going to do the opposite of what Covey states. We FIRST look for people to praise us and give us kudos, then we validate it with a pat on our own back. We also put too many expectations into man, which causes us to be disappointed repeatedly.

As the scripture says, keep on growing in knowledge and understanding in God as well as yourself. People will come and go in your lives, but their words will stay for an extended period of time. The words in the scripture are words God has spoken over your life. They hold so much more meaning and weight than anything someone else ever said about you or to you.

The way you instill His words within you is to read it daily, so it is ingrained in your spirit, your mind, and your heart. This way, you can stop looking for praise from others and celebrate yourself! You Matter. I need you to look in the mirror, tell the woman you see, "I Matter"! Open your mouth and provide yourself with a much-deserved affirmation to keep pushing and growing into the woman God called you to be. He already said it. You just need to believe it.

"What lies behind us and what lies before us are tiny matters compared to what lies within us."
– Ralph Waldo Emerson

Self-Reflections

Why do you matter? (Please be kind to yourself)
_____
_____
_____
_____
_____
_____
_____

In what areas do you want to grow your knowledge so you will grow?
_____
_____
_____

_____
_____
_____
_____

Positive self-declaration/affirmation for today:
_____
_____
_____
_____

Prayer

Lord, I thank you for the masterpiece you're creating in me. Now, I ask if you can help me grow in knowledge and understanding of me so I can fulfill the purpose you have in my life. I know I matter because you made me in your image! In Jesus' name, Amen.

Day 4- The Struggle

"and I am in deep distress. How long will it be? Turn and come to my rescue. Show your wonderful love and save me, Lord."
Psalms 6:3-4 Contemporary English Version

"You're never on time." "Why can't you ever keep things in order? "You eat like a horse!" "I can't believe you won!" "This is so simple. Why can't you understand?" The way we view ourselves is often disjointed and out of proportion. The struggle is real in some main areas, including weight, pleasing others, and accomplishing goals. When we hear those phrases, they are more often projections rather than reflections; projecting the concerns and character weaknesses of people giving the input instead of accurately reflecting who we are.

He knows you are going to struggle from time to time with a variety of events, people, and situations. But that is where you need to find strength in Him to get you through the rough patches. One of the evangelists at my church did a bible study on self-love. Her lesson included the Lotus Flower. This flower is white and pink, grows in shallow, murky water, roots are firmly in the mud, and sends out long stems where leaves are attached. It opens in the morning, and petals fall in the afternoon.

The year 2014 was a year of testing and growing my faith. In August of that year, I left a job I had for eight years without another job to go to because God said my time was up. In September of the same year, I was diagnosed with a very rare form of cancer that was in one of my salivary glands. Originally, it was a saliva stone that had gotten to the point of being unbearable in my left salivary gland, so surgery to remove it was scheduled. It was after they removed the gland, they found it was a tumor inside. It was nothing I would have ever imagined would have happened to me. During the next month, I obtained a new full-time job. But, during that time, I had to go to radiation treatments. That was a time of struggling to keep up with work, home life, all while being in a state of tiredness, pain, and weariness. I pleaded with God to please get me to a place of relief.

I eventually saw how He removed some things from my life in order for me to go through this ordeal. I then had a testimony to help others that had to go through a battle with cancer to give them hope. If I was still at the job I left in August of 2014, I probably wouldn't have ever had the surgery because I wouldn't want to miss work due to the workload I know would be waiting when I returned. What happened to me in 2014 has helped me to minister to women going through something this past year. As we grow, things will fall off us. We may be treading in muddy waters, but if we are rooted in our faith, great things will develop and blossom within your purpose. In the meantime, keep your focus on the promise He has for you. If we are obedient to God in the midst of our ordinary lives, the extraordinary impact is always possible.

"Growth begins when we start to accept our own weakness."
– Jean Vanier

Self-Reflections

What are you currently struggling with that is hindering you from a goal you have for your life?

_____
_____
_____
_____
_____
_____
_____
_____
_____
_____

Do you believe He will get you out of your struggle? Why or Why Not?

_____
_____
_____
_____
_____
_____
_____

_____
_____
_____
_____

Positive self-declaration/affirmation for today:
_____
_____
_____
_____

Prayer

Thank you in advance Lord for getting me through the muddy waters of life. I know I don't get it right all the time, but I pray you see my efforts. I pray my struggle takes me to my purpose. In Jesus' name, Amen.

Day 5- I'm Slipping

"Unless the Lord had helped me, I would soon have settled in the silence of the grave. I cried out, "I am slipping!" but your unfailing love, O Lord, supported me. When doubts filled my mind, your comfort gave me renewed hope and cheer."
Psalms 94:17-19 New Living Translation Version

The scripture itself would be enough today, but let's elaborate on this. Self-doubt can slip in regularly if you are not careful. It can cause self-sabotage, which causes you to belabor the actions that are needed to work towards your purpose. When life hits you, the momentum slows down and you slip back into your old ways. In June 2006, I got baptized again. Yes, I said again. My first baptism was at the age of five and I did not understand what I was doing. As a teen, I had the habit, as I explained in my introduction, looking for attention in men, and at this point, I came out of an emotionally abusive relationship. I was tired and needed a change. Getting baptized as an adult gave me a whole new perspective on life, God, and what was next for me.

In the digital age we live in, distractions cause us to lose our focus and let self-doubt come into the picture. If we're not careful, we start slipping again. I will work on something so diligently only to find myself engulfed in the latest and greatest going on within social media. I see how someone has launched their product or started a project that I was also thinking of doing. I often must go to the key verse of today and remember to cry out to Him when I feel myself slipping, drifting, allowing self-doubt to overtake my thoughts and my progression. Once you get the Word embedded in your mind, it will flow to your heart, and you start to feel the comfort of the Lord.

"The only person who can pull me down is myself, and I'm not going to let myself pull me down anymore."
— C. JoyBell C.

Self-Reflections

What have you slipped into?
_____
_____
_____
_____
_____

What distractions can you remove to get you back on track?
_____
_____
_____
_____
_____

_____
_____
_____

Positive self-declaration/affirmation for today:

_____
_____
_____

Prayer

Lord, I ask you today to hold on to me tight, so I won't slip too far from you. Forgive me for not coming to you first when I do drift and need a lifesaver to pull me back in. I want to draw closer to you so that I won't fall to the point of no return. Thank You for Your Grace. In Jesus' name, Amen.

Day 6- His Grace

"What should we say? Should we keep on sinning, so that God's gift of undeserved grace will show up even better?"
Romans 6:1 Contemporary English Version

First, let's thank Him for His Grace! We go through life making decisions, many times not consulting Him, and He continues to keep us. God is a God of second chances, mercy, and grace. However, let's not abuse His grace. Because He does grant us the grace as the scripture says, should we keep sinning? Of course not. You don't want to stretch or test Him like that. That is when it becomes abuse.

Appreciate His grace by conducting a self-evaluation of what can be done differently to not continue in the manner of sin. You must identify what your triggers are. Triggers are things that will lead you to sin. You will have temptations, but if you fill yourself with His spirit and stay away from the things that trigger you, as the scripture states, God's gift of undeserved grace will show up in your life. If He sees your intentions to do better and you are trying, He is pleased.

So how do you make it better? Pay attention. It sounds so simple, but why is it so hard for us to do it? Look closely at the warning signs and choose carefully. We don't want to take His Grace for granted. But guess what? He still can grant you grace, even if you have slipped and went back. He is ok with imperfect progress. As long as you get back on the right path, His grace is everlasting.

"Our self-respect tracks our choices. Every time we act in harmony with our authentic self and our heart, we earn our respect. It is that simple. Every choice matters."
— **DAN COPPERSMITH**

Self-Reflections

What choices do I currently need to make for my life?
_____
_____
_____
_____
_____
_____
_____
_____
_____

What has God given me grace over?
_____
_____
_____
_____
_____

_____
_____
_____
_____

Positive self-declaration/affirmation for today:
_____
_____
_____
_____

Prayer
Thank you for the grace you have put over my life thus far. I know I didn't serve it, and I am grateful. Please forgive me for not consulting you first when I make decisions in my life. I'm praying I talk to you more often to get your approval over my life. In Jesus' name, Amen.

Day 7- His Mercy

"However, when God, our Savior, made his kindness and love for humanity appear, he saved us, but not because of anything we had done to gain his approval. Instead, because of his mercy, he saved us through the washing in which the Holy Spirit gives us new birth and renewal."
Titus 3:4-5 God's Word Translation

You may be wondering what the difference between grace and mercy is. Mercy is withholding deserved punishment; grace is giving us what we don't deserve. Have you ever been in a situation where you could have been locked up, dead, or sick based on the actions you made but was able to just walk away with no repercussions? That is mercy! I have so many instances where He has granted me mercy. I talked about a toxic relationship I was in for five years. He gave me many signs that I shouldn't be in that situation, but my emotions got in the way of what reality was. The breaking point was when we got into a physical altercation. That was the first time he put his hands on me. But God granted me mercy because I had been ignoring what I was supposed to do. God saved me by giving me that wake-up call. As verse 5 says, He saved me through the washing in which His spirit gave me new birth and renewal.

That situation made me get a whole new perspective on life. Maybe you have been in a situation that He has granted you mercy. I am sure you have. Know that he granted that mercy to you so you can be renewed. Repent and ask for forgiveness, He surely will forgive you, and He will show up even better in your life.

"The wonderful news is that our Lord is a God of mercy, and He responds to repentance."

Billy Graham

Self-Reflections

What are some areas in which God has granted you mercy?

_____
_____
_____
_____
_____
_____
_____
_____
_____
_____
_____
_____

What can you do differently to change your perspective on a certain situation in your life that he has already granted you mercy over?

_____
_____
_____

_____
_____
_____
_____

Positive self-declaration/affirmation for today:
_____
_____
_____
_____

Prayer

Lord, I thank you for your mercy that you extend to me every day! Please forgive me for not acknowledging your presence in my life. I pray that I can break that cycle so I can live within Your will for my life. In Jesus' name, Amen.

Day 8- Safe Place

"I will be glad and rejoice in your unfailing love, for you have seen my troubles, and you care about the anguish of my soul. You have not handed me over to my enemies but have set me in a safe place."
Psalms 31:7-8 New Living Translation

In 2006 I made a decision that would change my life forever. I moved from my hometown of Philadelphia, to Virginia! I only knew two people but I secured a job, temporary housing, and had an amazing support system. My parents helped me along the way. Looking back at it now, I realize that God set me in my safe place by bringing me to Virginia. He saw the troubles I was going through and the road I was heading down. He observed the destructive behavior I was starting to display, which could have determined the fate of my children. After ending a toxic 5-year relationship, I started to go out to clubs more, drink more sociably, and hang out at after hours spots. I thought it was a way to discover my new freedom. But, that was not a road I needed to continue to go down. The night that changed everything was when I woke up the next morning at home but couldn't remember half of the night. Thank God I was with one of my girlfriends and nothing bad happened to me. But the fear that came over me about not knowing what happened the night before was enough for me to say, "something must give."

He protects you from your enemies, which at times, can be yourself. His love for you is unconditional so don't fret, He still loves you despite your downfalls. But you must be willing to let Him put you in that safe place. You will know it's a safe place when things start falling into place and favor falls upon you. A safe place is being in His presence, wrapped in His Grace, and feeling peace and joy come over you. So how do you get to that safe place? First, determine what you are trying to get saved from. Identifying what needs to be removed can help with the next step of what to go to God for in prayer. Next, surround yourself with positive people and positive thoughts. This can come through reading His word daily to give you that security of His presence over you. So, don't give up, seek Him so He can put you in that safe place.

"We should not give up and we should not allow the problem to defeat us."
- A. P. J. Abdul Kalam

Self-Reflections

What situation are you currently trying to get out of?

_____
_____
_____
_____
_____

_____
_____
_____
_____

What steps will you take to get to a safe place?
_____
_____
_____
_____
_____
_____
_____
_____
_____

Positive self-declaration/affirmation for today:
_____
_____
_____
_____

Prayer

Lord, please protect me from those that don't have good intentions for me. I thank you for removing me from the pain, places that are not good for me, so I can get into my safe place. Please cover me and protect me. In Jesus' name, Amen.

Day 9- Developing Endurance

"Not only that, but we rejoice in our sufferings, knowing that suffering produces endurance, and endurance produces character, and character produces hope."
Romans 5:3-4 English Standard Version

While writing this devotional, we continued to get more news and more results from testing of Covid-19. We began to live out, as my spiritual father, Dr. R.A. Vernon calls it, our "Temporary New Normal." I had to remember this will only make me stronger. The pandemic was making us use our critical thinking skills, get creative, and be more mindful of the life we live. As the scripture says, endurance produces character, which produces hope. We want to keep hope that things will get better.

Don't let those moments of the storm go by without drawing closer to Him. Drawing closer to God will assist in your endurance to get through some major milestones in your life. He wants your undivided attention, He wants you to seek Him for advice, not man. He wants you to be able to hear His voice so you can make sound decisions. Once you draw closer to him and get to the place of paying attention to his words, advice, and voice, you can gain the momentum necessary in those suffering times to get to your destination.

This is your chance to read more, write more, work on that business plan, that new venture so that when you are given the green light to come out of your situation, your suffering, or your storm, you can set things in motion and not miss a beat! I encourage you today to work on your endurance in this season, so when you hit the ground running, you won't lose momentum. If you push, God will pull it out of you. But in order to push, you have to run your race. You cannot run with weight on you, it slows you down. You have to let go of unnecessary weight.

"This is no time for ease and comfort. It is time to dare and endure."
- **Winston Churchill**

Self-Reflections
Think back and write down times of life that were hard that made you stronger.

_____
_____
_____
_____
_____
_____
_____
_____
_____
_____

_____
_____
_____

How can you continue to build your endurance to get through current storms or troubles?

_____
_____
_____
_____
_____
_____
_____
_____
_____
_____
_____
_____
_____
_____
_____

Positive self-declaration/affirmation for today:

_____
_____
_____
_____

Prayer
Lord, thank you for holding me up during my past troubles and hard times. Thank you for the strength to get through it as now I ask for strength to keep going, and keep my faith so I can get to the purpose you have for me. In Jesus' Name, Amen.

Day 10- Faith and Endurance

"Be assured that the testing of your faith [through experience] produces endurance [leading to spiritual maturity, and inner peace]. And let endurance have its perfect result and do a thorough work, so that you may be perfect and completely developed [in your faith], lacking in nothing."
James 1:3-4 Amplified Bible

Yesterday we touched on developing endurance during times of trouble. What about developing your faith along with your endurance? Whoa! A lot to handle, right? In January 2020, our church started a Bible study series on faith. You may not realize it, but we practice faith in various ways every day. When we drive our car, we don't think twice to look to make sure the vehicle is intact. We sit in a chair without checking to see if it is stable.

Faith is the substance of things hoped for. The formal definition of "hope" is a feeling of expectation and desire for a certain thing to happen. So that means you may not see it immediately. In order to see the perfect, complete thing God has for you, you have to build endurance to work through the past experiences and your present. You also have to build your faith. For some, that doesn't come easy, so taking steps to strengthen it is necessary. Trusting God is the first step. You have to trust He knows what is best for you as He knows your beginning and your end. Ask Him to build your faith. The more you converse with God concerning what you are longing for, the more you will start to see things manifest, which will build your faith. And one of the main things that will build your faith is enduring trials. When things look bleak, stay the course of strengthening the trust you have for Him and knowing He wants the best for you.

Enduring trials is like running track. In order to build your endurance to be able to run the upcoming race, even if you are a sprinter, for practice, they make you run cross country. Cross country is almost what it sounds like. You run long distances. Running the long-distance gets you ready for the big race! Oh, you should have shouted right there! The practice to build your endurance will give you a better chance to complete and even win the race! But you have to have faith that you will keep going until you get to the finish line.

"Faith is taking the first step even when you don't see the whole staircase."
-Martin Luther King, Jr.

Self-Reflections
Have you been tested in your faith? If so, how?

_____
_____
_____
_____
_____

_____
_____
_____
_____
_____
_____
_____
_____

What can you do to keep going until what you have faith for comes to pass?

_____
_____
_____
_____
_____
_____
_____
_____
_____
_____
_____
_____
_____
_____
_____

Positive self-declaration/affirmation for today:

_____
_____

_____
_____
_____

Prayer

Lord, help me to keep going in this season as I know you have better for me on the other side of this. I'm praying my faith grows and gets stronger as time goes on so I can win the race you have for me. In Jesus' name, Amen.

Day 11- Have Hope

"And this hope will not lead to disappointment. For we know how dearly God loves us, because he has given us the Holy Spirit to fill our hearts with his love." Romans 5:5 New Living Translation

Yesterday the definition of hope was given. It bears repeating today. The formal definition of "hope" is a feeling of expectation and desire for a certain thing to happen. So that means you may not see it immediately. I can attest to this. In June 2019, I was desperately seeking employment due to my hours being cut for the summer. My frustration grew more and more as I applied internally, had several interviews, including getting as far as 2nd interviews to come up without an offer. My husband sent me a text one day, "Lord, said, "Closed doors are only an indication of where you're not supposed to be. Thank Him for ordering your closed doors." This simple sentence gave me hope that something was better for me. As the scripture says, this hope will not lead to disappointment. I held on to the hope that God would send the right job my way, and He would not disappoint me.

Holding onto hope is the way to deal with the "No's." He didn't open that door because he knew where it would lead, which is not towards your purpose. You have to know that God loves you and knows what is best for you. If you feel like you have no hope, do a self-evaluation to really dig deep to see if that is true.

To give you an update on my job status, in November 2019, God placed me in the position that was right for me. I landed a work from home opportunity, which soon after showed that He has a love for me deeper than I realized. He knew the pandemic of COVID-19 was coming. He knew staying at that organization would have eventually led to me being laid off. So, hold on to hope because God loves and cares for you as He sees what lies ahead for your future.

"5 Signs You're Doing Better Than You Think You Are:
You're not the same person you were a year ago.
You've got goals.
You've experienced real hardships.
You have 1 or 2 close friends.
You know that God has great things in store for you."

-Jared Sawyer, Jr.

Self-Reflections

Take the time to write down the details for any or all of the "5 signs you are doing better than you think you are" that is mentioned in the quote above.

_____
_____
_____
_____
_____

_____
_____
_____
_____
_____
_____

If you feel like you don't have any or some of the 5, what steps are you 1going to take to get there?

_____
_____
_____
_____
_____
_____
_____
_____
_____
_____

Positive self-declaration/affirmation for today:

_____
_____
_____
_____

Prayer

Lord, I thank you for where you have brought me so far, but I want to keep my hope alive. Please help me to become better so I can have better. Thank you for the closed doors so I can receive what is best for me. In Jesus' name, Amen.

Day 12- Constructive Criticism

"Every part of Scripture is God-breathed and useful one way or another—showing us truth, exposing our rebellion, correcting our mistakes, training us to live God's way. Through the Word we are put together and shaped up for the tasks God has for us."
2 Timothy 3:16-17 The Message Version

Have you ever said to yourself, "If I knew then what I know now…….." Oh, but I sure have. Life is the best teacher at times. But do you know some things in life could be a bit easier if you use His word as your guide? Do we not follow the word because the Bible is too real or will literally put you in your place if you would utilize the scriptures?

The scripture says it is God-breathed, and it will shape us for the tasks God has for us. That includes teaching you the truth about yourself. It is hard to take constructive criticism from others, but what about from God? The definition of constructive criticism is the process of offering valid and well-reasoned opinions about the work of others, usually involving both positive and negative comments, in a friendly manner. In the scripture, it says the word is there to correct our mistakes and train us to live His way. This can be uncomfortable, so we usually stay in incorrect behavior because it is familiar. In November 2010, I visited what is now called "The City Church." Dr. Dimitri Bradley, may he Rest in Peace, spoke a word that struck me. Dr. Bradley stated, "If you feel uncomfortable in one place and comfortable in another, you need to go to the uncomfortable place."

If you don't know what to do in that uncomfortable place, ask God for help. In 2 Chronicles 20:12 Message version, it says, "We don't know what to do; we're looking to you." All you must do is add reading the word daily to your routine. You will find the tools needed to go through this thing called life. Don't be scared of the word, take constructive criticism, and let it help you find the truth in you, so you will know the right path to take.

"Some people don't like change, but you need to embrace change if the alternative is disaster."
- Elon Musk

Self-Reflections
What do you depend on for guidance in your life currently?

_____
_____
_____
_____
_____
_____
_____
_____
_____
_____

Find some scriptures that will help you and be a guide in your current season of life. List them below.

_____
_____
_____
_____
_____
_____
_____
_____
_____
_____
_____
_____

Positive self-declaration/affirmation for today:

_____
_____
_____
_____

Prayer
Lord, I want to listen and know your word so I can get to the purpose you have for me. Please help me to be able to take your constructive criticism in a positive way so I can make a positive change. In Jesus' name, Amen.

Day 13- Discipline

"Some people like to know things. And they want to know when they are wrong. But fools do not want to know when they are wrong. They hate it when someone tells this to them."
Proverbs 12:1 EASY English Bible 2018

As a child, I'm sure you couldn't stand when your parents would discipline you because you wanted to do what you thought was fun or the right thing. Little did you know it was to prepare you for what was ahead, not necessarily what was happening at the moment. Let's be honest, even as grownups, not too many of us like to be corrected. Yesterday we talked about constructive criticism. So, what's the difference? Discipline is to teach you right from wrong. God disciplines His children (you) to ensure you have wisdom in everything you do. Deuteronomy 8:5 states, "So keep in mind that the Lord has been correcting you, just as parents correct their children." The Bible also says in Hebrews 12:5-6, "But you have forgotten that the Scriptures say to God's children, "When the Lord punishes you, don't make light of it, and when he corrects you, don't be discouraged. The Lord corrects the people he loves and disciplines those he calls his own." Discipline is a muscle that you can build. It is not too late to start building that muscle.

You must come to the realization you can't grow and/or change without correction. It is done in love. If you are always right, what lesson will you ever learn? Even if you never played a sport, you know that a coach is there to guide, lead, and to give the team members discipline so they can give their best in the game. In this game called life, let God be your coach and provide you with the discipline of reading daily, praying daily, and living for your purpose. It is wise to know you need correction. I call it the conviction of oneself. God will be so pleased with your self-awareness as He only wants what is best for you. Remember that discipline is an expression of his love for you. As my spiritual father, Dr. R.A. Vernon, once said, "Success in life to a great extent is based on your ability and willingness to follow instructions."

"Real knowledge is to know the extent of one's ignorance."
-Confucius

Self-Reflections

What areas in your life do you need discipline?

_____
_____
_____
_____
_____
_____
_____
_____

_____
_____

List some steps you will take to become more disciplined in those areas.

_____
_____
_____
_____
_____
_____
_____
_____
_____
_____
_____

Positive self-declaration/affirmation for today:

_____
_____
_____
_____

Prayer

Lord, thank you for correcting me, even when I didn't realize it was for my good. Because of your mercy, I have been given another chance to become disciplined in areas of my life. Please help and guide me in the direction I need to go in my purpose. In Jesus' name, Amen.

Day 14- He Promised Me

"Everything he does is full of splendor and beauty! Each miracle demonstrates his eternal perfection. His unforgettable works of surpassing wonder reveal his grace and tender mercy. He satisfies all who love and trust him, and he keeps every promise he makes." Psalms 111:3-5 The Passion Translation

I used to have a problem with promises. Why? Because I had to patiently wait to see if the promise would be fulfilled and patience was not my strong suit. I started trusting in God's promises wholeheartedly when I moved to Richmond, VA. He led me there to start a new life, and I had very few obstacles when getting established there. Even with just having a discharged Chapter 7 bankruptcy four months before moving, I was able to rent a place to live, and a year later, I bought a home. One thing I made sure of was to find a church home. Through time and prayer, you will come to the realization that you must trust in God that the promise will be fulfilled if you keep trusting and loving Him.

Now, what do you do in the meantime? Remember how He has kept you, gave mercy, and granted you grace. He knows there may be times where doubt creeps in and you may begin to wonder if He is really coming back. So He gives the promise of His sure return and of His personal care to reassure you and calm your fears.

The beauty in His promises is that He will let them come to pass when you least expect or when you no longer impatiently wait for it. I was reading through one of my journals from 2010. One of my dear friends at the time sent me Habakkuk 2:2-3 Message version, which says, "And then God answered: "Write this. Write what you see. Write it out in big block letters so that it can be read on the run. This vision-message is a witness pointing to what's coming. It aches for the coming—it can hardly wait! And it doesn't lie. If it seems slow in coming, wait. It's on its way. It will come right on time."

My vision at that time was to take the steps I needed to obtain a career that would allow me to save money and become debt-free. I wanted to have a big home for me, my husband (I was in the first year of dating my husband) Chris, and our children. I wanted to be financially stable as well as spiritually stable. As of 2020, most of my vision has come to pass. I have my husband and my children in a house big enough for all of us, career, and spiritually stable (still working on financially stable and debt-free, but it is coming). So, don't fret, just be patient. Then you will see the full manifestation of the promises He has for you. Remember, He controls your future, so trust God to shape it according to his timeline.

"Failure is a detour, not a dead-end street."
- **Zig Ziglar**

Self-Reflections

List some promises you are waiting to come to pass. Have you prayed about it and wrote the promises down?

_____
_____
_____
_____
_____
_____
_____
_____
_____
_____

What will you do, in the meantime, until your promise comes to pass?

_____
_____
_____
_____
_____
_____
_____
_____
_____
_____

Positive self-declaration/affirmation for today:

_____
_____
_____
_____

Prayer

Lord, thank you for protecting me from dangers seen and unseen. You have given me grace so I can see the promises You have for me. So, I pray, in the meantime, I continue to love and trust you as you know what is needed for my life. In Jesus' name, Amen.

Day 15- How He Loves Me So

"God showed how much he loved us by sending his one and only Son into the world so that we might have eternal life through him."
1 John 4:9 New Living Translation

I love the song, "How He Loves" by Anthony Evans. It is such a calming and reassuring song. The chorus is simple but powerful, "He loves us oh how he loves us, oh how he loves us, oh how he loves!" As the verse for today tells us, He loved us so much that He had his son die on the cross for our sins! What greater love do you know? Growing up, we know the love of our parents, or whoever raised us, nurtured us, and provided for us. But what happens when you get to a place that a person can't help you? He is always there, whether you know it or not. He has shielded you from unseen danger and loves you in spite of anything you have done not pleasing in His sight.

So, if God can love you like that, why can't you value and love yourself? Someone may have told you differently, but God's opinion of you is what matters the most. Every human life is sacred, and God loves everyone!

We all have done something we are not proud of. God can use everyone and everything to bring about a good result. You may have gone left when you were supposed to go right, but because Jesus died for your sins, you are granted grace and mercy every day. His love surpasses our understanding and is unconditional, so let His love pour into you so you can also love yourself.

"To love oneself is the beginning of a lifelong romance."
- Oscar Wilde

Self-Reflections

List some things you love about yourself.
_____
_____
_____
_____
_____
_____
_____
_____
_____
_____

If you had a hard time listing above, what steps will help redirect your thoughts to get you to the place of loving yourself?
_____
_____
_____
_____
_____

_____
_____
_____
_____
_____

Positive self-declaration/affirmation for today:
_____
_____
_____
_____

Prayer
Lord, I know I have not shown my love for You or myself as I should. Thank you for your grace and mercy. Please help me to see the good in me and not the bad. In Jesus' name, Amen.

Day 16- God Remembered Me
"Then, God remembered Rachel, and God listened to her and opened her womb."
Genesis 30:22 English Standard Version

If you don't know the story, you may want to read about Leah and Rachel. You don't have to watch TV to get scandals, just look in the Bible. It's better than reality TV. Leah and Rachel were sisters married to the same man. If you start in Genesis 29 you will see where Jacob had fallen for Rachel, but in order to be with her and get her hand in marriage, he had to work for his uncle, her father. When the time came to get Rachel, the father tricked him and put Leah in his bed instead of Rachel. I guess there were no oil lamps or fire burning for him to see that the woman he was having a meeting with was not Rachel. The father tried to downplay it and say the eldest must be married first and used this man to get extra work out of him by not letting him marry Rachel for another seven years. The jealousy and competition amongst the sisters start in Genesis 29:31 when Leah starts having children back to back, and Rachel had none.

He remembered Rachel's longing and desire to have a child, and despite the obstacles she inflicted on herself by allowing her husband to sleep with the help so she could have children, He granted her mercy, and He remembered. It's ok to view other's lives for inspiration but not imitation. You can be inspired by how someone wrote a book, so it jumpstarts you to start. But God remembers you. He knows your desires, your needs, and your purpose. Trust that He remembers You.

"Out of difficulties grow miracles"
- **Jean de la Bruyère**

Self-Reflections

What are you trusting God for in the waiting?
_____
_____
_____
_____
_____
_____
_____
_____
_____
_____
_____
_____

Do you trust that He remembers You? Why or Why Not?
_____
_____
_____
_____
_____

_____
_____
_____
_____
_____
_____

Positive self-declaration/affirmation for today:
_____
_____
_____
_____

Prayer

Lord, I thank you for remembering me even when I get impatient. Help me to gain more patience in the waiting. Please forgive me for trying to go my own way. I want to be obedient to your word. In Jesus' name, Amen.

Day 17- You are Treasured

"For you are a holy people [set apart] to the LORD your God; the LORD your God has chosen you out of all the peoples on the face of the earth to be a people for His own possession [that is, His very special treasure]. "The LORD did not love you and choose you because you were greater in number than any of the other peoples, for you were the fewest of all peoples."
Deuteronomy 7:6-7 Amplified Version

Are you in a place where you feel unappreciated? You give and give, and some show they are grateful, but most do not? I am here to tell you, woman of God, you are loved, and are God's treasure. He knows and sees your heart; your labor will not be in vain. There is a real medical condition of burnout. According to the World Health Organization, burnout isn't just synonymous with being stressed out. It's "a syndrome conceptualized as resulting from chronic workplace stress that has not been successfully managed."

If you are in a state of burnout, do an evaluation of your life, your job, and your friends. Be careful and do not let anyone take advantage of you. As Proverbs 2:11 says, "Wise choices will watch over you. Understanding will keep you safe." Seek him in ALL your choices, pick your best yes. The key to dismantling emotionally draining activities is getting the proper self-care and disconnecting from the day-to-day. You MUST find time to get your mental state in order. Remember, you are his daughter, His treasure in which he cherishes. You need to think about yourself the same way. If you have a problem with keeping yourself accountable, get an accountability partner who will push you to self-care.

"Please all, and you will please none."
-Aesop

Self-Reflections

Do you know how to say "No"? Why or Why Not?
_____
_____
_____
_____
_____
_____
_____
_____
_____
_____
_____
_____
_____

How many times per month do you practice self-care? If you don't, what plan will you put in place?
_____
_____

_____
_____
_____
_____
_____
_____
_____
_____
_____

Positive self-declaration/affirmation for today:
_____
_____
_____
_____

Prayer

Lord, I want to ensure that I treasure myself as you do. Give me the strength to only give my best yes, and practice self-care. As I know, I am your daughter. A father doesn't like to see their child in disarray. I thank you for comforting me and having me set apart. In Jesus' name, Amen.

Day 18- Soul Ties

"Don't you know that your bodies are part of the body of Christ? Is it right for me to join part of the body of Christ to a prostitute? No, it isn't! Don't you know that a man who does that becomes part of her body? The Scriptures say, "The two of them will be like one person." But anyone who is joined to the Lord is one in spirit with him."
1 Corinthians 6:15-17 Contemporary English Version

The scripture and quote for today are powerful! The definition of soul ties is when you spend time with someone to the point your soul combines. This does not always mean love. This could be everyone you have ever let too close to you mentally and intimately. Imagine EVERYONE you loved or THOUGHT you loved is trapped inside you? Can you say toxic? You inhaled souls that were no good for you. Have you ever felt like you were suffocating emotionally? The definition of suffocation is to feel or cause to feel trapped and oppressed. That is when you need to exhale and release them before you choke!

In my first real relationship, I was verbally and emotionally abused. I wasn't being suffocated physically, but I was emotionally. The soul ties were so strong that every time I said I would leave, it didn't last long and I went right back to him. At the time, I thought it was love, but looking back, I now realize it was unhealthy and was killing me mentally and emotionally. God gave me signs to tell me I needed to leave him, but I didn't pay attention. The soul ties overtook my rational thinking. I even had a pastor prophesy that whomever I was with was not the one for me! Of course, at that time, I wasn't in a place spiritually to accept something like that, so I ignored it.

After my first long and toxic relationship, I finally ended it when he put his hands on me. I always had the signs (Holy Spirit) I needed to leave him alone, but I didn't until the physical altercation. DON'T WAIT UNTIL GOD LITERALLY KNOCKS YOU ON YOUR BEHIND TO LISTEN TO HIM. Pay attention to the signs so that your soul doesn't get tied to the wrong person. This is for relationships with friends as well. Try to define what that relationship should be, an assignment (temporary or short term to teach you a lesson or help someone), or an authentic life long relationship.

"For so many years, I couldn't understand why every time I thought that someone finally loved me, like… for real, they would eventually turn to vapor. Every person whom I've ever loved is trapped inside of my chest. I've breathed all of them in so deeply that I've nearly choked and died on every soul that I've ever given myself to."
― **Jennifer Elisabeth, Born Ready: Unleash Your Inner Dream Girl**

Self-Reflections

What soul ties do you need to be released from?

_____
_____
_____
_____
_____
_____
_____
_____
_____
_____

How can you get soul ties with Christ instead?

_____
_____
_____
_____
_____
_____
_____
_____
_____
_____

Positive self-declaration/affirmation for today:

_____
_____

Prayer

Lord, I want to be wiped clean of my past soul ties. Please help me and guide me to be able to start anew and protect my soul from toxic relationships and those that are not for me. Help me to remember that I am yours, and you never want me to be tied to the wrong person. In Jesus' name, Amen.

Day 19- Saving Myself

"Promise me, O women of Jerusalem, by the gazelles and wild deer, not to awaken love until the time is right."
Song of Songs 2:7 New Living Translation

Yesterday we talked about soul ties and what it can do to you internally. When you have a sense of being wanted or needed, you can easily get to a place of desire and connect to any relationship, whether it is healthy or not. If you are not careful, you are quick to look for attention and love from others instead of God. Truth be told, looking back in my years before marriage, I didn't love myself enough to know it was ok to be alone and not need validation from others. Even though I have only been in a serious relationship twice in my life, I never liked being alone. So, I would fall hard for guys when they didn't reciprocate the feeling. It wasn't until the age of 30 that I became content with being by myself. You don't have to go down the same path I did. Save yourself for the right person who is going to love and cherish you, flaws and all.

You must value yourself before you expect that from others. Wendy Blight, the author of "I am Loved," wrote, "Sometimes rejection is God's protection." Sometimes you have to suffer temporarily to get the love that is right for you. If you want to be set apart, you will have to be moved away from things that will tempt you. So today, remove the thought that he didn't want you because you were not good enough. Might I suggest God was protecting you from hurt, harm, or even destruction? That is why it is very important to wait and not rush into relationships. Wait until the time is right so you will be able to receive love in a healthy way.

"The hunger for attention is usually a result of low self-esteem and the lack of unconditional self-love."
— **Edmond Mbiaka**

Self-Reflections

What relationships have been removed from your life that you now realize were not for you?

_____
_____
_____
_____
_____
_____
_____
_____
_____
_____
_____
_____
_____
_____
_____

Positive self-declaration/affirmation for today:
_____
_____
_____

Prayer

Lord, thank you for protecting me from relationships that were no good for me. My prayer is that I can have self-control and wait for the one you have for me. Thank you for loving me enough to put rejection in my life. In Jesus' name, Amen.

Day 20- Overflow of His Love

"Then you will be empowered to discover what every holy one experiences—the great magnitude of the astonishing love of Christ in all its dimensions. How deeply intimate and far-reaching is his love! How enduring and inclusive it is! Endless love beyond measurement that transcends our understanding—this extravagant love pours into you until you are filled to overflowing with the fullness of God! And I pray that he would unveil within you the unlimited riches of his glory and favor until supernatural strength floods your innermost being with his divine might and explosive power. Then, by constantly using your faith, the life of Christ will be released deep inside you, and the resting place of his love will become the very source and root of your life."
Ephesians 3:16-19 The Passion Translation

There is a little more scripture today because the words provided have a great depth of encouragement that we all need. Knowing His spirit dwells in you is a critical piece of knowing who you are. Many times, you know, but do you believe it? As the scripture says, His love pours into you, but you must be willing to receive it.

Within the scripture is a prayer. That prayer is that Jesus wants you to be overwhelmed with His love, glory, and favor. He wants nothing but the best for you. I know you think if He wants nothing but the best for me, why do bad things happen? There can be several reasons why. It could be to make you stronger or to make your story a testimony to help someone else. But do know, His love overflows to the point it flows throughout your inner being so that it will comfort and protect you.

"Love... it surrounds every being and extends slowly to embrace all that shall be."
- Khalil Gibran

Self-Reflections

Take a few minutes to write down what you believe to be true about God's love for you.

_____
_____
_____
_____
_____
_____
_____
_____
_____
_____
_____
_____

Positive self-declaration/affirmation for today:
_____
_____
_____
_____

Prayer
Lord, thank you for your overflow of love for me. Even when I don't acknowledge it, you still bring me favor. And I pray that you would unveil within me the unlimited riches of your glory and favor until supernatural strength floods my innermost being with Your divine might and explosive power. In Jesus' name, Amen.

Day 21- He Rescued Me

"But I trust in your unfailing love. I will rejoice because you have rescued me. I will sing to the Lord because he is good to me."
Psalms 13:5-6 New International Version

Have you ever bumped into an old flame and said, "Lord, what did I see in them?!" Have you thought to yourself, "Thank you, Lord, for RESCUING me!" This goes back to our main scripture. God knows what is and is not good for you, so He will rescue you when you don't even realize that is what's happening.

Maybe you don't need rescuing from someone else. You might need rescuing from yourself. Too many people seem to believe they are not allowed to put themselves first or go after their own dreams out of fear of being selfish or sacrificing others' needs. I was listening to "Do It Again" by Elevation Worship one morning while walking on the treadmill. I just went into worship through dance and tears! Then God said, "Stop worrying and start doing life," meaning live your life day by day and stop obsessing over tomorrow as God got this!

Think back to all those situations you were able to get out of. That bad and/or abusive relationship (whew child I had to shout myself on that one) or that stressful job. You were able to walk away from a bad accident with no scratches or bruises. Let's reflect on the verse of the day, "I will rejoice because you have rescued me!"

Maybe you haven't gotten out of that situation yet. Depend on God's ability to handle a situation instead of your own ability. Please know that God hasn't forgotten about you, and He is good to you if you let Him in so that you can be good to yourself.

"Freedom is nothing but a chance to be better."
- Albert Camus

Self-Reflections

From what situations do I need to be rescued? (Do you mean removed or rescued?)

_____
_____
_____
_____
_____
_____
_____
_____
_____
_____

How has God worked well out of the bad things that have happened to you or the bad things you've done?

_____
_____
_____
_____
_____
_____
_____
_____
_____
_____
_____
_____

Positive self-declaration/affirmation for today:

_____
_____
_____
_____

Prayer

Lord, I thank you for always thinking of me, being good to me, and being a God of my blind spots. Thank you for rescuing me from dangers seen and unseen so I can start to walk in your purpose. In Jesus' name, Amen.

Day 22- Plans for Me

"I know what I'm doing. I have it all planned out—plans to take care of you, not abandon you, plans to give you the future you hope for."
Jeremiah 29:11 The Message Version

As a teenager, I was very much interested in fashion. I even took fashion design/sewing as part of my high school curriculum for a year. I went on to go to a college for fashion merchandising. But as life went on, my plan was not God's plan. As I mentioned in my introduction, I am currently in ministry, something I would have never planned for my life, but God knew where I needed to be. In July 2014, I had a great position and was earning very good money, but I was drowning in mental burnout and was experiencing overwhelming anxiety every time I went to work. The current acting Director had a meeting one day with us, and she stated, "There will be some major changes coming (there were changes every week). Either you can stay on the boat and go with us with the changes, or you can get off the boat." God spoke to me at that moment and said, "Get off the boat; your time is up." I had a huge struggle with making the decision to leave; so much so, I cried off and on for days. I was grappling with the fact that God wanted me to leave a job without another one to go to. Eventually, I put my notice in. I realized God put that plan in place so I could draw closer to Him, restore my faith, and get prepared for the next season in my life.

God knows what is going to happen before it happens. He has strategically designed your life and where you will end up. However, we can, at times, drift from His plan and go by our plans. But He knows what is best for us. He has given us all free will and the ability to make our own choices. He wants you to go the route less traveled. Travel the route that allows you to be your authentic self. As the scripture says, He has it all planned out. He will take care of you and not abandon you. We often feel like He abandoned us, but He never leaves our side. We are the ones that stray away from Him.

It's ok to dream, but know it takes action and prayer for it to come to fruition. So, know He has planned a bright future for your life, just let Him lead you there.

"To accomplish great things, we must not only act, but also dream; not only plan, but also believe."
- Anatole France

Self-Reflections

What is a dream you have?
_____
_____
_____
_____
_____
_____

_____
_____
_____
_____
_____

What steps have you taken to make your dream a reality?

_____
_____
_____
_____
_____
_____
_____
_____
_____
_____
_____

Positive self-declaration/affirmation for today:

_____
_____
_____
_____

Prayer

Lord, I need your guidance. At times I feel like I am at a stop sign and don't know where to turn. Please direct me in the path I need to go that is within the plans you have for me. In Jesus' name, Amen.

Day 23- Your True Self

"Since God chose you to be the holy people he loves, you must clothe yourselves with tenderhearted mercy, kindness, humility, gentleness, and patience."
Colossians 3:12 New Living Translation

As a young adult, I had a temper. Why? I believe it was due to how I was treated in elementary school. When I was quiet, people picked on me to the point I got in a lot of fights. When I got older, I decided I was not going to be quiet anymore. I was quick to argue or confront a problem, and I had very little patience. Those attributes caused me some hard times later in life because I did not always demonstrate the best behavior when facing certain situations.

From time to time, we must be reminded of today's verse. Changing your mindset and actions can make a world of difference in your life. If you break down the scripture in this way:
1. Mercy- We want God to grant us mercy, but we don't extend the same to our neighbors, co-workers, church members.
2. Kindness- Treat people as you want to be treated
3. Humility- This is one of the best attributes to have. It shows wisdom, discipline, and honor to God.
4. Gentleness- Being gentle in how you react and respond to something can make a

conversation or a situation turn around for good.
5. Patience- This is a big one! We all have times where we are going through a rough day or week. This causes a lack of patience. We want people to be patient with us and grant us grace, so why not do the same for others?

Let's apply today's scripture to our lives so you can transition to your true self within God. Four practical truths to begin making a transition to your true self:
1. Pay attention to your inner being in silence and solitude- journal with prayer how you're feeling without censorship.
2. Find trusted companions - ask God to bring persons in your life that can help you pull back the layers to get you closer to being emotionally healthy
3. Move out of your comfort zone
4. Pray for courage and be willing to tolerate the discomfort necessary for growth.

"Have patience with all things, but, first of all, with yourself."
-Saint Francis de Sales

Self-Reflections

What areas do you need to improve in; Mercy, Kindness, Humility, Gentleness, and/or Patience?
_____
_____

_____
_____
_____
_____
_____
_____
_____
_____

What steps will you take to improve those areas?
_____
_____
_____
_____
_____
_____
_____
_____
_____
_____

Positive self-declaration/affirmation for today:
_____
_____
_____
_____

Prayer

Lord, please help me to be better to myself as well as others. Even if someone is not so kind, gentle, patient, or merciful toward me, let me be more like you. Give me the strength to improve in the areas I exposed so I can be better and learn my true self. In Jesus' name, Amen.

Day 24- I Got the Power

"Lord, I passionately love you and I'm bonded to you, for now you've become my power!"
Psalms 18:1 The Passion Translation

Where do you get your energy from? Is it through exercise, socializing, or retreat? Think about that for a moment. When you become mentally drained, how do you regain your energy? The best way to do this is by getting power through the source, which is the Lord. In order to get the power from Him, you must be connected. In order to be connected, you need to have a relationship with him, so he recognizes your voice. Connect with him when you first get up in the morning. That connection can make your day more positive, give you the energy to push through, and allow you to have peace. My connection time is in the shower. It is a place that is sacred so I can just focus on Him. Others may have a prayer room or a certain area around the house to do this. It doesn't matter where it is. Just find a place. Maybe you connect with him better when you listen to some music and take a walk.

Another way to connect with Him is to connect to others that are connected. Evaluate who you have in your life that has an intimate relationship with God. They can provide spiritual guidance and advice. Lastly, get up and move. Once you start moving, there is power in your footsteps. Jesus doesn't align himself with lazy folk. He provides power to those that try to start going.

His power that lives in you will shine through you if you let it. Believe it or not, you have an influence on others, so you must let His light shine so they can see Him in you. Your testimony will give someone else a source of power. They may get the courage to go to a therapist, go to the doctor, or start their business. Remember, to keep going and striving as His power in you will give you strength when you are weak.

"If you realized how powerful your thoughts are, you would never think a negative thought."
- Peace Pilgrim

Self-Reflections
What do you believe to be the current source of your power?

_____
_____
_____
_____
_____
_____
_____
_____

What is a testimony you can share to give someone the power of hope?

_____
_____
_____
_____
_____
_____
_____
_____
_____
_____
_____
_____
_____
_____
_____
_____
_____

Positive self-declaration/affirmation for today:

_____
_____
_____
_____

Prayer

I Love you, Lord, as You are the source of the power within me. I will no longer be afraid, for You are with me. I won't be discouraged, for you are my God. Please strengthen, help, and hold me up with your victorious hand. In Jesus' name, Amen.

Day 25- Hate on Me

"'The people who belong to this world may hate you. But remember this: They hated me before they hated you. If you belonged to this world, this world's people would love you. They would love you because you would belong with them. But I chose you so that you would be separate from this world's people. You do not belong with them, so they hate you."
John 15: 18-19 Easy English Bible 2018

We are always saying, "We have haters." We associate the phrase with people not being happy for our success or accomplishments. Haters speak negatively and try to destroy what you have accomplished. It is ok to have haters. The scripture tells us the world will hate you because you are not of the world; you are of God. However, you must realize that if you make positive moves, you will get positive results. It is all in how you react to the action and words of others. If you are moving and doing something, someone is going to talk about you, which is free advertisement. In 2011, I got a position as a supervisor. I believe I was the youngest supervisor in the department. Even though it wasn't said to me directly, there were employees that had negative opinions because I was young and in a management position, while some of them had been there for years. I never let the "comments" that would surface from time to time get to me. Why? Because God placed me there, not man. God saw my potential and decided I was right for the job.

You have unique characteristics that no one else has nor would they understand. Because of this, they will talk, and may have negative things to say. God intended for you to stand out from the rest. If you never had someone in your life that didn't like you, then you aren't doing something right. Some people hate your presence because you represent power. There will be opposition, especially when you are working for your purpose. The closer you get to your destination, the more you will come against, naysayers, "haters," and negative people. Stand tall, keep your head up and keep striving to your destination.

"If you have no critics, you'll likely have no success."
- Malcolm X

Self-Reflections

Where are you heading? What is your destination?

_____
_____
_____
_____
_____
_____
_____
_____
_____

What will you do to ensure "haters" don't block you?
_____
_____
_____
_____
_____
_____
_____
_____
_____
_____
_____
_____

Positive self-declaration/affirmation for today:
_____
_____
_____
_____

Prayer

Lord, have pity on me as my enemies chase me. Many of them are pursuing and attacking me, but even when I am afraid, I keep trusting You. I praise You because I know you will not anyone harm me. When I pray, Lord, my enemies will retreat because I know for certain that you are with me. In Jesus' name, Amen.

Day 26- I've Got Confidence

"Be happy in your confidence, be patient in trouble, and pray continually."
Romans 12:12 God's Word Version

Rejoice! I know you are thinking, "For what? Right now, I don't know if I'm supposed to go left or right. Currently, my life is a mess. I'm living paycheck to paycheck." We all go through something from time to time, but in order to be confident in hope, you must have faith. One of my greatest fears years ago was failing; failing my children as well as myself. Whenever I didn't finish something, I felt like a failure because I was used to finishing what I started. That struggle was between my head and my heart for a long time. Through life experiences, God brought me through trouble and pain. Paired with continuous prayer, the confidence that you can keep going with His strength will build positivity in your life.

It is important to keep positivity and be patient as help is coming. Through prayer and faith, anything is possible. Miracles, signs, and wonders are possible. You may not have experienced this yet, but if you have confidence in God, your perspective will change. The key to having faith, hope, and confidence again is to pray. You may be saying, "I don't know how to pray." Think of it as a conversation with God. Just let Him know the matters of your heart. As you start to build your confidence in prayer, you will build your confidence in hope and faith.

"Inaction breeds doubt and fear. Action breeds confidence and courage. If you want to conquer fear, do not sit home and think about it. Go out and get busy."
– Dale Carnegie

Self-Reflections

How often do you talk to God?

_____
_____
_____
_____
_____
_____
_____
_____
_____

What can you do to build your confidence in prayer, faith, and hope?

_____
_____
_____
_____
_____
_____
_____
_____
_____

_____
_____
_____
_____

Positive self-declaration/affirmation for today:
_____
_____
_____
_____

Prayer

Lord, I want to have the confidence in You as well as myself. Please guide me and be patient with me. I will continue to keep praying even in times of trouble as I know better is coming. In Jesus' name, Amen.

Day 27- Speak into My Life

"Don't say anything that would hurt [another person]. Instead, speak only what is good so that you can give help wherever it is needed. That way, what you say will help those who hear you. Don't give God's Holy Spirit any reason to be upset with you. He has put his seal on you for the day you will be set free [from the world of sin]. Get rid of your bitterness, hot tempers, anger, loud quarreling, cursing, and hatred."
Ephesians 4:29-31 God's Word Version

Do you often indulge in negative self-talk? You need to be careful what you speak into your own life as well as others. If we are not careful, we can become our own worst critic. I know you have heard this millions of times, but you need to understand the seriousness of being more self-conscious about how you perceive yourself. "Those who control their tongue will have a long life; opening your mouth can ruin everything."
Proverbs 13:3 NLT

I used to be a part of the dance ministry at one of the largest churches in Richmond, VA. As a member of the team, I was stretched beyond what I thought I was capable of. In April 2014, we were preparing for a program. The leaders asked us to fast a month before. We were also tasked with journaling our experience. I went back and read it, only to discover, I was not kind to myself. But I was very transparent with God. Some of the content stated, "on my skin surface, I see stretch marks, dark spots on my face, and a big stomach. I'm always trying to hide my stomach because I don't like how it pokes out, and people think I'm pregnant. Beyond the skin surface, I am depressed at times but don't want to seem like I am weak." Reading how I viewed myself then and looking at where I am now has helped me to help other women with their self-esteem and speak life into them.

Some people are existing and not living. God will move in us to accomplish the work He has planned for us. God sees our potential even when we can't and considers us worthwhile just the way we are. He is consistent even when we are not.

"What you are shouts so loudly in my ears I cannot hear what you say" **Emerson.**

Self-Reflections

How would you describe yourself if you didn't have fear and/or rejection in your mind?

_____
_____
_____
_____
_____
_____
_____

_____
_____
_____
_____
_____
_____
_____

Positive self-declaration/affirmation for today:
_____
_____
_____
_____

Prayer

Lord, I don't see myself as one with potential. I've done too many things unworthy of Your confidence in me. But I want to see it differently. I want to believe the impossible. Help me see what You see and speak into my life so that I can have the same confidence as You do in me. In Jesus' name, Amen.

Day 28- Live in Peace

"Christ has given you peace in your minds. So, let that peace rule your thoughts. God has chosen you to be like one body, as his people. So he wants you to live together in peace. Thank God for everything that he gives to you."
Colossians 3:15 Easy Bible 2018

As children, many of us didn't have a care in the world. We lived for the moment, carefree, and with no worries. Now, as adults, we must be more intentional about letting peace rule our thoughts, while eliminating worry. Remember, we will not live eternally on earth. So, the brief time we are here, we need to utilize our time wisely. Your mind is a precious instrument that is tied to your wellbeing. Don't clutter it with unnecessary stress and people.

And maybe it's just me, but when I clear out my closet, clean my room, or clean my bathroom, I feel a sense of a clear mind because of my clear space. I feel free from clutter and filth. If you continue to live in filth and clutter, your thoughts will stay cloudy. You will remain stuck because you can't move around the clutter. If you clear some things out of your life, you begin to think clearly. You have to stop hoarding others' issues as it is stunting your growth! You can be a listening ear or help to those in need, but you cannot carry and hold their burdens. Set your mind free from clutter and live in peace.

The entire premise of decluttering is based on increasing your ability to love on yourself and gain peace. This will also give you the ability to be clearer on the choices you need to make in life.

"We can never obtain peace in the outer world until we make peace with ourselves."
- **Dalai Lama**

Self-Reflections

List things that have robbed you of your peace.
_____
_____
_____
_____
_____
_____
_____
_____
_____
_____
_____
_____

What are some things you need to remove from your life, to gain peace?
_____
_____
_____

_____
_____
_____
_____
_____
_____
_____

Positive self-declaration/affirmation for today:
_____
_____
_____
_____

Prayer

Lord, thank you for giving me peace in my mess. Help me to discern what I need to remove from my life to have continuous peace. Let peace reside in me so I can handle the situations that come to me in this world. In Jesus' name, Amen.

Day 29- I Got the Victory

"The one who loves us gives us an overwhelming victory in all these difficulties."
Romans 8:37 God's Word Translation

Have you ever gone to start your day with Jesus and Coffee, read your devotions, and have the conversation with God that you are not going to let stuff get to you?
The things you also say to yourself:
1. You are going to be positive when others are negative.

2. You are not going to take everything personally.

Well, your intentions are great, and then something or someone comes along and tests your confidence, your positivity, and your religion: doubt and a feeling of being overwhelmed starts to creep in. You know what I am talking about. And sometimes it's not people; it's situations that arise that disrupt your thoughts, your plans, and even your courage. But as the scripture says, despite all those things, those thoughts, the situations in your life, you have the victory. Make up in your mind that you will overcome that thing that tried to hold you back. Repeat after me, "I am an overcomer!"

Once you recognize you are an overcomer, you can claim victory! You can claim victory over your circumstances, your job, and your finances. One of the most important things is claiming victory over your life! You are almost a month into this devotional, and I decree and declare that you have overcome doubt of your self-confidence, your self-worth and found the power that is within you to go to the next level. You got the victory!

"God has already done everything He's going to do. The ball is now in your court. If you want success, if you want wisdom, if you want to be prosperous and healthy, your going to have to do more than meditate and believe; you must boldly declare words of faith and victory over yourself"
-Joel Osteen

Self-Reflections

What are some thoughts or situations you need to overcome?

_____
_____
_____
_____
_____
_____
_____
_____
_____
_____

_____
_____

List some things you have overcome and got the victory!

_____
_____
_____
_____
_____
_____
_____
_____
_____
_____

Positive self-declaration/affirmation for today:

_____
_____
_____
_____

Prayer

Lord, I thank you for shifting my mindset to embrace the victory I have over my life. My past troubles and situations will not define me, as I am an overcomer due to your strength within me. When I start to falter, you bring me back up to victory! In Jesus' name, Amen.

Day 30 - Future Glory

"I consider that what we suffer at this present time cannot be compared at all with the glory that is going to be revealed to us."
Romans 8:18 Good News Translation

There is this song I found through Pandora, and it's called, "No Bondage" by Jubilee Worship. The chorus is so powerful as they say, "There is no bondage, every chain is broken. There is no bondage. Jesus our hearts are open. No guilt, no shame, all my sins are erased." I used to think the things I went through were not significant because others have been through worse. Holding on to my testimonies didn't feel like I was guilty or shameful. But, I came to realize it was keeping me in bondage.

Once you realize you are in bondage, you need to release and tell your testimony. Believe it or not, what you went through is to help someone else. Something good is going to come out of the storm you are in or have been in.

When you get out of the bondage, you can also finally see the real you. You must go through some things, some trials, and tribulations in order for Him to get the glory out of your life and for you to get to your future glory. It will not be comfortable. You must get out of familiarity to experience greater.

I love the message version, which says, "That's why I don't think there's any comparison between the present hard times and the coming good times. The created world itself can hardly wait for what's coming next." This journey I'm currently on is not comfortable at all for the introverted person I am. What you have going on presently is not what the future may hold. But this is the plan God has for you, and there will be glory after this!

"Stop pretending and start becoming."

-Dr. Victory Vernon

Self-Reflections

Who are you trying to become?

_____
_____
_____
_____
_____
_____
_____
_____
_____

What do you need to let go of so you can allow yourself to grab a hold of what is in store for you?

_____
_____
_____
_____
_____
_____
_____
_____

What does future glory look like to you?

_____
_____
_____
_____
_____
_____
_____
_____

Positive self-declaration/affirmation for today:

_____
_____
_____

Prayer

Lord, you have gotten me out of bondage and given me a clear path to start walking in my purpose. Please reveal to me the steps and resources I need to get there. I thank you in advance for what is next. In Jesus' name, Amen.

Appendix A

My prayer is that this devotional has helped you in some way. The hope is to touch all women, young & seasoned, all races, and ethnicities. Even if it was just one day that gave you a breakthrough, I am thankful. I am thankful that God saw fit for me to go through what I went through to help you. Don't hold on to this blessing. Bless someone with a copy of the devotional so we can spread women's empowerment across the globe! If you need a daily reminder after reading this devotional, use the Empowerment Wall below and place it on a poster, in a frame, and put somewhere you can see it. So if you are having a difficult moment or day, you can review it and see what you need to do to get you back on track.

Empowerment Wall

Create a poster or use multiple sticky notes to write the items listed below. Find something to put in an area you often see in your home.

1. Take a slow breath. Continue for 3 min.
2. Drop your shoulders and do a gentle neck roll.
3. Call or email a friend you haven't talked to in a while.
4. Turn your negative thoughts of an outcome into a positive thought.
5. Allow time to pass to reduce anxiety without doing things that increase your anxiety.
6. Think about what is going RIGHT in your life.

7. Do things you enjoy calming you down.
8. Watch your favorite comedy show or movie, something that will make you laugh.
9. Cuddle up with your favorite pet, a friend, or family member.

About the Author

Shawniece Moore is a wife, mother, stylist, and motivational speaker with a big heart for women. Her transparency, boldness, and sensitivity show through her writing and speaking. Overcoming years of self-esteem and self-worth issues is a testimony of victory as she continues to inspire those that hear her speak. She is the founder and creative director of Uniquely Complex, who motivates and encourages women to defeat self-doubt and walk into their purpose. She also has her own apparel line of self-love shirts. She assists her husband, Dr. Chris Moore, in ministry at New Kingdom Christian Ministries in the poverty-stricken neighborhood of Highland Park in Richmond, VA. There, she leads the women's group "Virtuous Women of Faith" as well as the praise dance ministry "Envision Dance Ministry."

If you want to connect with Shawniece for motivational speaking, workshops or to purchase of self-affirmation t-shirts:

Website: www.uniquelycomplex.com
Facebook: www.facebook.com/1unquelycomplex
Instagram: @1uniquelycomplex
Twitter: @complexuniquely

References

1. Blight, Wendy. **I am Loved.** Thomas Nelson 2017
2. Brown, Dalvin. **Burnout is officially a medical condition, according to the World Health Organization** USA TODAY May 2019 https://www.usatoday.com/story/money/2019/05/28/burnout-official-medical-diagnosis-says-who/1256229001/
3. Covey, Stephen R. **The 7 Habits of Highly Effective People: Powerful Lessons in Personal Change.** FranklinCovey Co. 2017
4. Kaiser, Shannon. **The Self-Love Experiment: Fifteen Principles for Becoming More Kind, Compassionate, and Accepting Yourself.** TarcherPerigee 2017
5. Scazzero, Peter. **Emotionally Healthy Spirituality.** Thomas Nelson 2011
6. Song excerpts from "No Bondage" by Jubilee Worship
7. Song excerpts from "How He Loves" by Anthony Evans
8. Quotes mentioned in this devotional were retrieved from BrainyQuote Application.
9. Scriptures retrieved from YouVersion Bible Application

www.ingramcontent.com/pod-product-compliance
Lightning Source LLC
Chambersburg PA
CBHW030223170426
43194CB00007BA/836